# EDUCATION FOR A FREE SOCIETY

*By* HOMER E. COOPER

*Cost of Training Teachers*

*Education for a Free Society*

DR. HOMER E. COOPER
1877–1953
*College Administrator*

# EDUCATION FOR A FREE SOCIETY

FREEDOM COLLEGE AND
OTHER ESSAYS ON EDUCATION

## BY HOMER E. COOPER, Ph.D.

*Edited by Clara Chassell Cooper*

*An Exposition–University Book*

EXPOSITION PRESS          NEW YORK

Exposition Press Inc., 386 Fourth Avenue, New York 16, N.Y.

**FIRST EDITION**

*TO*

## DR. HOMER E. COOPER

As Dean of the faculty
The wise counselor and able instructor
As Chairman of the Rules and Regulations
  Committee
The zealous exponent of clean sportsman-
  ship
As Chairman of the Course of Study Com-
  mittee
And the greatest hope for their wise solu-
  tions
Who, giving his life of unselfish service
To every good cause that he could promote
Has gained the admiration and gratitude of
  the faculty as well as the whole student
  body.

**DEDICATION**
Reproduced from *The Milestone*, 1927, published by the Senior College of the Eastern Kentucky State Normal School and Teachers College,
Richmond, Kentucky.

# FOREWORD

*Education for a Free Society* is a collection of educational essays which grew out of Dr. Cooper's wide experience as a college administrator, and his recognition of a lack of sincerity of purpose and a similar lack of consistency of practice in numerous educational situations that he observed.

*Freedom College,* which constitutes Part One of the book, proposes a remedy for this insincerity of purpose and inconsistency of practice. By means of a Prospectus of Freedom College, he charted the course for a new type of college which he hoped to establish, an educational institution that should be noteworthy for its spirit and practice of academic and intellectual freedom.

In seeking the means to establish such a college, he wrote, "There is nothing more enduring in human affairs than an institution of higher learning, well-established and well-managed. Such an institution may reasonably be expected to carry on an active career of many centuries." He recognized that colleges which succeeded in continuously justifying their existence had outlasted governments and even nations, and he confidently believed that the founders of the new type of college which he designated *Freedom College* would be creating for the ages.

*Other Essays on Education,* constituting Part Two of *Education for a Free Society,* further illustrate Dr. Cooper's educational philosophy by concrete applications in a variety of situations, including the liberal arts college, the teachers' college, general education, professional education, and intercollegiate athletics.

CLARA CHASSELL COOPER

*Berea College, Berea, Kentucky*
*July 1, 1957*

# CONTENTS

PART TWO
*Other Essays on Education*

*Part One*

---

## FREEDOM COLLEGE

## EDITOR'S NOTE

THIS PROSPECTUS was written by Dr. Homer E. Cooper in 1937 while he was Dean of West Liberty State Teachers College. Because of general financial distress in the country and the beginning of World War II, conditions would have been unfavorable during that period for the establishment of the new type of college called for in the prospectus. After the war the need for such a college continued; and thus the manuscript, essentially unaltered, was mimeographed and copyrighted in 1952 as a means of making it available to foundations that might be interested in affording the project financial backing. It has never been publicly distributed.

At the time of his death in January, 1953, Dr. Cooper was actively engaged in efforts to establish Freedom College by attempting to secure funds, to clarify its tax-exempt status, and to set up an Advisory Body, as initial steps in its organization. Although efforts to establish the college were necessarily terminated, the need for such a college had increased, rather than diminished. Moreover, it was believed by persons who read the manuscript that Dr. Cooper's plans for Freedom College should be made public.

In this revision, incorporating a number of verbal changes made by the author, and other minor alterations, the prospectus is now being presented to a wide professional audience, in the hope that other educators may be challenged to complete the unfinished task of establishing Freedom College as an institution that shall be noteworthy for its spirit and practice of academic and intellectual freedom.—C. C. C.

# INTRODUCTION: THE NEED FOR A NEW TYPE OF COLLEGE

## *Lack of Objective in Present-Day Colleges*

HIGHER EDUCATION in the United States is in a bad way. The colleges are like sheep without a leader. Apparently they have no continuing or consistent purpose to give them a sense of direction; in practice each one strays hither and yon. At any one time they seem to be heterogeneous in their activities, although the apparent differences are usually in the adjuncts of the college only; yet over a period of years each traverses about the same paths as each of the others has traversed. Indeed, it is a rare college that does not traverse many of them at the same time. That is, the practices of a college at any one time may be inherently widely diverse, and as contrary as all the practices of the colleges are.

The inherent incongruity or incompatibility of practices carried on concurrently by a given college are illustrated in the three examples cited below, which have come under the observation of the writer:

1. In one college, made up of approximately sixteen departments which hitherto had exercised little autonomy but among which there had been a commendable degree of co-operation and a minimum of inter-departmental jealousy, the administration proceeded abruptly to give a large and questionable degree of autonomy, a degree for which no appreciable need was felt, and at the same time without warning or consultation to promulgate a paper organization on the "division" plan, one after the pattern then being adapted to the liberal arts curriculum at the University of Chicago.

2. An institution gave much lip service to high standards of scholarship; but when it came to cases, every decision was determined by the prospect of immediate, although frequently temporary and sometimes illusory, popularity.

3. Faculty members in one college were exhorted in faculty meetings to "fail" all unpromising students, but again and again students who were palpable failures were encouraged and even urged to re-enter, even in cases in which the records contained no intimation of desirable studentship.

Similar practices might be cited in large numbers. Certainly such inconsistency is conclusive as evidence that the colleges employing these practices have no sense of direction. Not only that, but this inconsistency brings into question the integrity of their administrators.

## *Pressure on Faculty Members to Make an Impression*

MANY FACULTY MEMBERS of the present day are working at a low intellectual level because of fear engendered by the mandates of their official superiors. Officials such as presidents or deans require them, sometimes tacitly but not infrequently by definite command, to do something which will attract attention—the attention sought being that of the ignorant. In some cases the penalty for lack of response is loss of position. It is frequently a withdrawal of the privilege of salary increase. Whatever the penalty, fear and other types of uneasiness are set up, all of which act as effective deterrents to productive intellectual processes and to stimulating teaching.

The mandates are of many kinds. Only a few need be mentioned. One of those most frequently applied is the requirement to produce, which means that the staff members in most departments must publish, whether they have anything worth publishing or not. An immediate result is the appearance of a large amount of printed rubbish.

Teachers of music and of drama are required to produce programs. The results are frequently painful, as would be expected.

Teachers in practically all fields are squeezed into the mold of the Master of Arts degree or that of Doctor of Philosophy. It matters not that the requirements for the degree may be unsuited to the tastes or the needs of the faculty member. Higher degrees are thought by administrators to be good talking points, and the nickname "Doctor" appeals strongly to the tongue; therefore, the more higher degrees the better.

## *Where the Emphasis Needs to Be Placed*

THE LOW-PRICED AUTOMOBILE, supplemented later by the bus, enabled more young people to reach high school within the first quarter of this century than had any other one facility in the century preceding. It also enabled many to reach college. The educational trend continues, although the automobile is no longer low-priced.

The automobile has enabled the individual to reach the high school or the college *physically*. It is now time for the young to be enabled to attend college *intellectually*. This can be done by the creation of a college that deals with intellectual matters.

## *The One Way to Create a New Type of College*

THE CREATION OF a new college is the only practicable means of creating a new *type* of college. It may seem at first thought that the way to bring about the new type of college is to transform one already existing; on second thought, the practical difficulties become apparent and the historical evidence becomes conclusive.

In the first place, a college already in operation has a staff which, as a whole, is adjusted to current practices and which gives a large measure of approval to them.

In the second place, the alumni as a body are accustomed to think of their alma mater as having always been nearly ideal, and consequently they stoutly oppose significant change.

In the third place, the lessons of history are to the effect that important changes, when brought about at all, come so slowly and at the cost of so much turmoil and such a disruption of the work of the institution that they might better not be brought about at all. Examples that might be cited are McGill University, the University of Redlands, and St. John's College, all in the 1930's, and West Virginia University in an aggressive administration around the beginning of this century. When a movement to bring about small changes, such as those proposed for the colleges just mentioned, produces the degree of paralysis which they experienced, it seems improbable that such a college would survive a marked change, to say nothing of a transformation.

In opposition to any thought of large change, it should be observed that any college is likely to continue for several generations much as it began. While in time it may enter the graduate field, its essential nature remains the same. Examples may be seen in Oberlin College, Yale University, Antioch College, Washington and Lee University, Berea College, and Amherst College.

It is easily possible to create a new type of college. Two conditions are crying for it.

In the first place, great numbers of people want it. They do not constitute a majority of the people, but in the aggregate they are a very large and a very important element of the population. They want the kind of college that will give them the opportunity to acquire sound scholarship and omit the unimportant digressions. In other words, they are earnest people who are famishing for basic ideas, but who recognize the typical college as an uneconomical place to acquire these ideas because of its greater emphasis on less important matters. They realize that the usual period of four years spent in college ought to provide an opportunity for a kind and degree of scholarship far more important and far more thoroughgoing than is usually afforded by the college.

In the second place, while the existing faculties generally are reconciled to current practices, and generally approve and consequently would make drastic change impossible, yet there is a serious-minded element increasingly restive because of lack of opportunity under existing conditions to be of service to young people, and as a result ardently desiring a transformation. The number of these people is sufficient to provide staffs for many colleges. The opportunity is most inviting to organize a faculty of superior attainment, ideals, and leadership by procuring one member here and another there, a majority of these from existing faculties, some from business, professional, and literary fields, and some from the student members of the graduate schools.

# FREEDOM COLLEGE: A PROSPECTUS

THIS PROSPECTUS proposes the formation of a new type of college which shall avoid many of the shortcomings of present-day colleges. To emphasize its independence and its untrammeled nature, this college is designated *Freedom College.*

The distinctive nature and the general plan of Freedom College are defined in the following pages.

## 1. PURPOSES

THE PURPOSES OF Freedom College may be briefly stated as follows:

1. To give students an opportunity to study, to receive instruction, to observe processes and movements at first hand, to test out hypotheses, to assemble data, to acquire experience, and to arrive at conclusions.
2. To serve as a source of information and intellectual guidance for the citizenry, when called upon.
3. To serve as a sanctuary for individual study by persons not registered as students.
4. To promote scholarship in the staff itself.
5. To afford intellectual companionship to faculty members and to others who may seek it.
6. To set a scholarly example to other institutions.
7. To apply or try out promising procedures in college administration, curriculum, character-building, processes of instruction, or any other worthy enterprise which is appropriate to the college level of studentship.

It is contended by many factions of society that colleges should fire their students with a zeal for action to this or that end. In the case of some, the end is the creation of a new social order. In the case of others, maintenance of the existing social order and thwarting the agitator is the end. In one group the promotion of a given creed is paramount; in others, tolerance and co-operation are practices *par excellence.*

If all the wishes of all the factions could be operative in all the colleges all the time, every college would be doing every thing and in every way defeating its every purpose. It would generate much heat but no light.

The intention of Freedom College is not to incite but, in contrast, to afford the means of insight.

If history teaches anything, it teaches that government, social structure, religious belief, and human thought will change. If it teaches anything, it teaches that some of this change may be advantageous and some disadvantageous. Again, if it teaches anything, it teaches that knowledge directed by good judgment—which consists essentially of knowledge seasoned by experience—is required to bring out the good and avoid the bad in change, whether of kind or tempo.

## 2. SCOPE

### Level

*Freedom College is designed to serve the nonprofessional, nonvocational area between the secondary and the graduate schools.* It will not offer teacher training nor other professional or vocational instruction; and it will never enter upon graduate instruction as such—with this provision: that it will give graduate courses if the graduate schools of the country place barriers in the way of students who desire to pursue graduate study after having studied in Freedom College, the graduate courses to be withdrawn as soon as seems practicable after such barriers have been removed. While the college will thus exclude vocational and professional instruction as such, the instruction in basic fields which will be available will be applicable to teaching, engineering, statecraft, the law, medicine, the ministry, music, art, literature, industry, commerce, and practically every other pursuit.

In the founding of Freedom College as a purely nonvocational college, there is no intention to disparage vocational education either by overt statement or by implication. On the contrary, it is recognized that in the case of many vocations education directed to that end is one of the quickest and most economical ways of preparing the individual for effective work.

While this is true, it is likewise true that nonvocational education is required to promote understanding—that is, understanding of events, social movements, and trends in whatever field, even including vocational trends.

The purpose is, therefore, to recruit the student personnel of Freedom College from those who have ability and a disposition to acquire understanding and who feel that they can take time for its acquisition for a few months or years before entering upon immediate preparation for a vocation.

It is to be expected (as stated elsewhere) that the higher degree of understanding fostered by Freedom College will indirectly contribute much to vocational wisdom as well as to satisfaction; and, in teaching as a vocation, this understanding will make a large contribution to that fullness which is essential to the really good teacher, but which is lacking in many who assume that they are teachers.

### Territory Served

GEOGRAPHICALLY, the college will be national or international. The admission officers may exercise their judgment as to whether an individual ought to be admitted, but no geographical lines will be drawn unless conditions warrant such action as a temporary measure.

The location of the college should be such as to serve the purposes already stated and to foster the cosmopolitan character of the institution. It should therefore be within easy reach of an important governmental center, either national or state, such as the seat of the national government or that of a large and populous state. It should likewise be within easy reach of highly industrialized and commercialized centers and of important agricultural sections.

## 3. DIFFERENCES BETWEEN FREEDOM COLLEGE AND THE TYPICAL COLLEGE

To EMPHASIZE at the outset certain distinctive characteristics of the proposed new type of college, the differences between Freedom College and the typical college are listed in parallel columns:

| *Freedom College* | *The Typical College* |
|---|---|
| 1. The promotion of understanding, scholarship, integrated and co-ordinated knowledge, an understanding of the relations of facts—in short, wisdom—will be kept uppermost in the selection of students both for entrance and for retention and in the whole conduct of the college. | 1. The promotion of appearances and of superficial knowledge not infrequently consumes much of the energy of the administration and staff. |
| 2. Educational value will be put before publicity value. | 2. Educational value is frequently sacrificed to publicity value. |

| *Freedom College* | *The Typical College* |
|---|---|
| 3. Permanent values will be put ahead of temporary values; that is, a sound educational program will be followed. | 3. Getting the "scoop" or advantage by a succession of temporary expedients or opportunistic shifts is the practice. |
| 4. The president will be recognized as just a high-grade college man, and no attempt will be made to parade him as a wonder man. The prominence will be given to the teaching members of the staff. | 4. The president is frequently exalted to a degree entirely unjustified either by attainment or ability, is asked to give addresses on numerous occasions, whether or not he has anything to say, his statements being heralded by the public as oracular utterances, and generally has his time so filled by outside engagements as to preclude any serious attempt at scholarship or long-range planning for the college. At the same time, able members of the staff are almost entirely obscured. The president not only acquiesces in these practices but encourages them. |
| 5. The administrative officers will recognize that their primary function is to enable students to study and teachers to teach. They will therefore resist the tendency to use students for parade purposes and teachers for trivial and temporary jobs presented by the whim of the administrator. | 5. Students are frequently paraded and shown off, and teachers are frequently treated as mere puppets. No opportunity is given for a staff member to pursue a continuous and constructive plan of teaching. |
| 6. Not only will able staff members be selected, but an attempt will be made to use their abilities in the most productive | 6. Often the assignment of courses to staff members is made without consulting any of them as to the courses in which |

*Freedom College*

*The Typical College*

way by assigning them to the teaching duties that they can do best.

7. Prescribed curricula in the sense of a minimum amount of credit in this subject or a minimum amount of credit in that will not be followed. The student will be expected to form the habit of supplementing his obvious and guided study by reading and observing to the extent of attaining breadth. He will also be expected to become markedly proficient in one or more fields. In fine, he will be expected to attain a marked degree of scholarship in at least one field, and have in addition a large fund of accurate and meaningful information in a wide range of fields.

8. The student will be expected to bring to the college or to acquire in residence a taste for a considerable number of recreations and sports of a kind that may be practiced after leaving college, and to participate consistently in such activities while in college.

9. The students, and the faculty for that matter, will be encouraged to engage in the games usually classed as athletics and to play in contests. No attempt will be made in such

their abilities can be applied to best advantage.

7. A given amount of credit, distributed as prescribed, equals a degree. A degree equals an education.

8. The worth of any student is proportional to the attention he attracts, whether the activity is adapted to post-college practice or not.

9. A few students are over-trained for a restricted number of contests in a limited number of sports for the purpose of winning championships. Intramural sports are perfunctory

## Freedom College

games and contests to conform to association restrictions as to the opening and closing of seasons, the number of contests per season, or the kinds of teams with which matches should be played.

10. Instruction in the games will be available when asked for, but no official coaches will be provided, and no records of games will be kept.

11. Petty penalties, such as "campusing," will not be imposed, nor will petty and detailed rules be laid down. It will be assumed that the satisfactory student will conduct himself in a way that is tolerable. Any who do not so conduct themselves will be eliminated. With respect to conduct, and in fact many other matters, advice will be easily available and obtainable when asked for, but it will not be imposed.

12. Only students of high ability and desirable industry will be sought, and only those who manifest these qualities after entrance will be retained.

13. Sincerity of purpose, integrity of achievement, and intellectual honesty will be regarded as *sine qua non* in the student and the faculty member.

## The Typical College

and not widely practiced. The opportunity and equipment for a wide range of sports are almost always lacking.

10. Instruction is now enforced and pressure is put on the promising athlete to participate. Favorable records are widely heralded.

11. Students are subjected to petty restrictions unworthy of an organization of adults and humiliating to mature young people. Student government, if permitted at all, is usually limited to trivial matters.

12. High-pressure recruiting is practiced.

13. Selling pseudo-wisdom is a common practice.

| *Freedom College* | *The Typical College* |
|---|---|
| 14. Faculty meetings will concern themselves with the large and permanent problems of the college. | 14. Faculty meetings have a tendency to concern themselves with temporary problems and trivial matters. |
| 15. Faculty members will be encouraged to produce when they have anything to produce, but verbal rubbish will be discountenanced. | 15. Faculty members are often required to produce as a means of promotion or retention, and verbal rubbish or drivel is accepted, acclaimed, and proclaimed. |

## 4. PLAN OF TEACHING AND CURRICULUM

### *Elasticity Provided For*

THIS PROSPECTUS is purposely silent on many issues, among them detailed aspects of plan of teaching and curriculum. The reasons for silence in regard to such matters require only to be mentioned in order to be seen.

Colleges that continuously justify their existence outlive governments and even nations. It should therefore be clear in the minds of the founders of Freedom College that they are creating for the ages. The college must adjust itself to the governmental, economic, social, scholastic, and moral development of the environment.

Since no man can foresee with certainty these developments even for a generation, the college must be free from far-reaching provisions of such nature as to hinder this adjustment, but, on the contrary, must be given freedom to act on the good judgment of its responsible officers, after the purpose is clearly stated and after safeguards are set up to render inoperative certain influences which, when operative, have always proved destructive.

## *Fields of Instruction*

IT IS NOT the intention of the college to give instruction in any field merely to serve the purpose of opportunism, the whim of the controlling body or that of the president or other staff member or group of staff members, nor will popular demand which seems to be ephemeral lead to instruction in any field. On the contrary, the offerings will be made up of such fields and courses as seem, after careful consideration, to serve a relatively permanent and continuous need.

Furthermore, no field will be entered unless or until the college has sufficient resources to provide library, laboratory, staff, supplies, and other requisites adequate as a whole to a high-grade undertaking in the field.

Any or all of the fields usually touched at the college level may be entered, when such entrance is consistent with the purposes already stated. In addition, provision will be made for exploration and creativeness in practically any field for which the student has a bent.

### *Divisions of Work to Be Undertaken in the Immediate Future*

THE DIVISIONS in which instruction should be offered from the beginning or the opening of the college are the following:

I. RELIGION

Bible Literature
Comparative Religion
History of Religion
Philosophy of Religion

II. SOCIAL SCIENCES

History
Economics
Sociology
Recreation and Health
(individual and community)
Political Science
Psychology
Philosophy
Archaeology
Geography
Ethics
International Relations
Contemporary Thought

III. LANGUAGES AND LITERATURE

| | |
|---|---|
| English | Latin |
| French | Russian |
| German | Spanish |
| Italian | |

IV. FINE ARTS

| | |
|---|---|
| Music | Home Decoration |
| Painting | Drama |
| Sculpture | Dance |
| Creative Art (in such media as wood, leather, clay, and metal) | Aesthetics |

V. SCIENCE

| | |
|---|---|
| Mathematics | Geology |
| Physics | Biology |
| Chemistry | Astronomy |

## 5. HINDRANCES TO STUDY AND TO THE PROPER FUNCTIONING OF A COLLEGE STAFF

IT IS PROPOSED that Freedom College apply its energy and talent to the major functions of a college, which are stated in the list of purposes. To this end it is intended that the college shall avoid certain hindrances to study and to the proper functioning of a college staff, some of the more common of which are enumerated below. Certain of these hindrances act as direct obstacles, while others reduce the effectiveness of instruction by shifting the emphasis from important to unimportant functions.

### 1. *Credits, marks, degrees*

Freedom College will keep careful records of the studentship and achievement of the student and of his life in the college, but will not give hours of credit nor assign marks until such time as it is felt that the public can understand the meaning of credits and marks and a staff can assign and the student receive credits and marks as evidences of opportunity for education rather than as constituent parts of an education. In other words, credits and marks will be eliminated until our conceptions change to the extent that such an expression as "an education" will no longer be used.

All degrees conferred will be honorary in nature rather than "earned"—that is, will be an expression of recognition by the college of real achievement in some field—and will be restricted to persons who have studied in Freedom College.

## 2. *Assembly (misnamed chapel) exercises consisting mainly of drivel*

Either chapel for the purpose of worship or convocation for the purpose of any worth-while discussion may be an important part of the activities of a college; but the kind of so-called chapel that is usually carried on not only wastes the time of the student but is highly destructive to the ideals appropriate to college studentship.

## 3. *Too much activity and too many activities*

Instructor and student are frequently too busy (usually doing little things) to do anything except be busy.

## 4. *Too much teaching as such and too little study by either staff member or student*

Even a little observation in libraries and laboratories reveals that faculty members and students do not study. Such observation further reveals a superficiality of knowledge, an ignorance of the relationships of facts, and an absence of the habit of reflective thinking on the part of both instructor and student that is appalling.

## 5. *Attempts to attract attention*

These attempts express themselves in numerous ways, including an excessive amount of public speaking on the part of the president and members of the staff, the publication of articles that make no contribution to knowledge or thought, radio discussion and entertainment participated in by staff and students, high school visitation by orchestra or other student groups, excursions to impress the public with the bigness of the institution rather than for increased knowledge, and many others. Not infrequently they destroy the opportunity to study for one or more days. In some cases they appear periodically throughout the year and persist through many years.

## 6. *Pretense*

Pretense manifests itself in many ways. Occasionally it consists of a misinterpretation or a misrepresentation of statistical or other data. Not infrequently it is an assumption of superior wisdom or knowledge on the part of president or staff. Often it consists of exaggeration and a persistent attempt to make a small achievement look like a large one. Perhaps most frequent of all is an appearance of excessive friendliness or interest in the welfare of a student. Needless to say, in any institution there are some faculty members and some students who recognize lack of sincerity when they see it. Confidence, morale, and genuine studentship are frequently prevented from developing, or are destroyed if already developed, by a resort to pretense on the part of persons to whom the students should look for example and guidance.

## 7. *Apparent conformity to the beliefs of administrative officers or donors*

Such appearance of conformity is frequently maintained for the sake of promotion in rank or other advantage to accrue to the staff member, for the advantage of a "stand-in" on the part of the student, or for the sake of a prospective donation on the part of the administration or of the institution as a whole.

8. *Autocratic shaping of policies and offerings by an administrative officer (president or dean) who wields official rather than scholastic authority*

This practice has varieties too numerous to describe, but it is frequently exercised to the extent of making the teaching members of the staff mere errand boys for the administration.

9. *The idea that all students and faculty members should do the same thing at the same time, and should become enthusiastic simultaneously and whenever called upon to do so*

Typical requirements are that all attend chapel, lectures, " 'thuses," athletic contests, convocations, and the like, and be active participants in "pep" meetings and other manifestations of the type of college spirit that expresses itself mainly in "rahs."

10. *The exaltation of the president, resulting in the relative debasement of the staff*

This exaltation is practiced by governing boards, by the public, by favor-currying staff members, and in newspaper publicity, as well as in the salary schedule. The president is called on to make a very large number of speeches, and frequently it is assumed that he represents the college and speaks for the college, when in fact it is a rare president who is sufficiently studious and scholarly and who does enough broadgauge thinking to enable him to do better than misrepresent the scholarly aspects of the institution.

## 11. *A costly plant and a cheap staff*

This is one of the most common and most detrimental ways of misplacing emphasis in American colleges.

## 12. *The distraction of conferring honors*

This frequently takes the form of Founders' Day, the dedication of John Doe Hall, or convocations honoring distinguished visitors (who may or may not be distinguished). There are many current practices of such a nature by which the college gets considerable publicity through the press and otherwise for which it pays nothing directly, and which may be classed as prominent means of attracting attention. It is really important for students to come into contact with distinguished people and to become well acquainted with their ideas and to evaluate them dispassionately. Convocations for the purpose of enabling students to become acquainted with such people can be made highly beneficial to the students. When that is the purpose, such events are to be commended rather than condemned.

## 6. SAFEGUARDS TO FREEDOM

To ensure the carrying-out of the purposes of Freedom College, a number of safeguards to freedom are suggested:

(1) The college shall not bear the name of a family, a region, a political unit, or another institution, nor shall the campus, any building, any equipment, any chair of instruction, any donation, any organization within the college or in any way connected with it, or any other part or feature of the college bear such a name. However, an official post office and other

service offices, such as a transportation center and express office, which may be established for the convenience of the college community after the college has procured a location, may take the name *Freedom College* or any appropriate combination of that name. Likewise, the college community or neighborhood may exercise the same privilege.

Furthermore, at some appropriate place on the campus a memorial to the donor or donors may be provided. It is expected that the memorial will be well maintained, enduring, and in good taste, and that it will be in all respects of such a nature as to inspire in students and others reverence for the purposes and respect for the generosity and self-denial of those who made the college possible.

(2) The college shall not associate itself with any organization by membership, affiliation, alliance, or any other relationship, nor shall any organization, committee, club, fraternity, department, or any other part of the college do so. Any club, fraternity, or other organization that seems appropriate may be organized in connection with the college, but no local chapter, branch, or other feature of any exterior organization shall be organized or exist on the campus or in connection with the college, even though located off the campus; and no body after having been organized shall associate itself with any exterior body.

This restriction shall not be applied in such a way as to prevent the college from conducting or sponsoring one or more preparatory schools; nor shall it prevent individual staff members or students from carrying membership in organizations exterior to the college.

On the other hand, this section shall be interpreted to mean that Freedom College will decline membership in regional standardizing agencies and all other exterior organizations—scholastic, athletic, social, fraternal, or other—and that all parts of the college will do likewise; that Freedom College will set its own standards, and that all parts of the college will proceed harmoniously with this principle.

(3) Any donation to the endowment or to a permanent fund shall be made without specific purpose and without designation, such as the name of the donor, shall be merged in the general endowment or trust fund for the use of the college, and shall surrender its identity, as in the case of the general endowment or trust fund.

Specific contributions to current expenditures (not to capital outlays or permanent fund) may be made for any year and the purpose of the expenditure designated, but no such contribution shall be renewed in whole, in part, or in any modified or disguised form more than one time, and the total amount of time covered by such contributions shall not be more than two fiscal years.

(4) There is a tendency (very human but nevertheless very detrimental to high ideals) observable in the operation of colleges which causes the administrative officers to be ever on the alert for additions to endowment, plant, and income, and to shape instruction in the light of any prospect. There is, furthermore, a belief, often expressed and more often acted upon, that an institution must increase in size. It will be regarded as a specific duty of the Advisory Body and the faculty to resist both of these tendencies.

To ensure that the size of the college will be determined in the light of the purposes which it seeks to serve, the Advisory Body will set a suitable figure (as 600 or 1,200) as the maximum enrollment, and will prescribe that this maximum shall not be exceeded.

At intervals of a few years the Advisory Body will define the scope of the college and determine the adequacy of the income in terms of the work to be undertaken. Whenever in the judgment of the Advisory Body the income is adequate, the

Body will serve formal notice of adequacy on the Board of Trustees; whereupon the Board of Trustees will decline to accept further donations.

(5) The college shall maintain at all times the spirit of academic and intellectual freedom, and shall avoid scrupulously any impairment of such freedom because of apparent financial or institutional obligation. The full spirit of Safeguards 1 to 4, above, shall be operative.

## 7. PERSONNEL

### Board of Trustees

(1) There shall be a Board of Trustees of seven members, whose duties shall be financial only. The original members of this Board shall be appointed by the major donor to the trust fund and confirmed in accordance with law. This Board shall be self-perpetuating except in the case of the president of the college, who shall be *ex officio* a member and whose successor shall be appointed as hereinafter provided.

(2) The Board shall hold title to all property belonging to the college, and shall have the right to acquire or convey titles, in harmony with the purposes of the college and the laws of the state in which the college is situated.

(3) The Board shall handle and invest all trust funds and make available for the current use of the college the income from such funds.

(4) The Board shall make available for the current use of the college such other income, as tuition or gifts for current expenditures, as may accrue from time to time.

(5) The Board shall make available for the use of the college each year all the income of that year, except as provided in *a* and *b* following.

*a*) It shall systematically and regularly save up a reserve over each of the first sixteen years of the operation of the college, excepting the first year, which shall at the end of the sixteenth year amount to the full yearly cost of operating the college, so that the college could if necessary operate undiminished the seventeenth year without income.

It shall maintain this reserve intact against depression, to be used only in times of clearly defined financial depression; and when any part of it is used, it shall be restored as soon as practicable when the depression is passed.

Furthermore, if the annual expenditures of the college increase in years subsequent to the sixteenth year, it shall augment this reserve by an amount that will keep it equal to the budget for the current year.

*b*) If at the end of any fiscal year (September 1) there is on hand from income an amount in excess of the amount necessary to pay the bills of the closing year, the excess shall be invested and become a part of the trust funds, except that an amount not exceeding 10 per cent of the total income for the year may be set aside as a reserve specifically for buildings, equipment, library materials, or other such purposes.

(6) The Board shall see to it that expenditures within any fiscal year shall not exceed income, except as authorized in Provision 5.

(7) The members of the Board shall give surety bond covering honest handling of the funds.

(8) The members of the Board shall be jointly and severally responsible for keeping the trust funds intact and unimpaired, and invested in only such securities and property as are appropriate and legal for savings banks and legal fiduciaries, except that when such securities are extraordinarily high in price relative to income, the Board may invest an amount of the trust funds not exceeding one-third of the total in other securities or property, provided that such investments may be made only on unanimous vote of the Board (record of which must be

made in the minutes), and provided further that any investments so made may continue not to exceed six months unless
continued by unanimous vote of the Board.

(9) The members of the Board shall be reimbursed for their
expenses incurred because of meetings of the Board, but shall
receive no other fees or salaries.

## Advisory Body

(1) There shall be set up in the provision of the trust an
Advisory Body, the original members of which shall be appointed by the major donor to the trust fund. This Body shall
include the president of the college, who shall act as chairman,
and six other members, who shall not be employees or in any
way financial beneficiaries of the college.

(2) Any vacancy, other than that of the chairmanship,
which may occur in the Advisory Body shall be filled as follows:

*a*) Names may be proposed by any member of the Body or by the
faculty.
*b*) In voting for new members, the present members shall each
have one vote, and the faculty by representatives duly selected
shall cast six votes.

(3) It shall be the duty of the Advisory Body to elect the
president and, on his recommendation, the faculty and other
employees and to fix the rate of compensation, provided that
the major donor in setting up the trust fund may appoint the
first president, state his salary, and fix a term of years for that
appointment.

It shall be the duty of the Advisory Body to determine
the policies of the college in harmony with the provisions of
the trust and the purposes of the institution, to consider questions of policy with the president or with the president and
official representatives of the faculty, and to raise questions

regarding policy for consideration by the Body, the president, and the faculty.

It shall be the duty of the Advisory Body to maintain working relations based on good will with the president and the faculty. Whenever such relations can no longer be maintained, it shall be the duty of the members of the Body other than the president to file their resignations, to become effective when their successors shall have been chosen and qualified, but such resignation shall not create ineligibility to election. An election shall then be held without delay. If, when the members of the Body as so elected shall have qualified, the Body is still unable to maintain a satisfactory working relation with the president and the faculty, then it shall be the duty of the Body to reassign duties among members of the staff or to remove members thereof, after reasonable notice, until it can maintain such a relation, provided that the president appointed in the original plan may not be so removed nor his duties modified without his consent during his term of office as fixed by the major donor to the original trust fund.

(4) It shall be the duty of the Advisory Body to acquire by purchase, gift, lease, construction, or other means, adequate and appropriate land, buildings, equipment, libraries, privileges, rights, and other facilities to carry out the purposes of the college.

In the case of any facility procured in the discharge of this duty, title shall be vested in the Board of Trustees.

### Staff

(1) The staff shall consist of a president, a faculty, and such other officers or employees as may from time to time be provided for.

(2) The president shall be the executive officer of the college. He shall determine, subject to approval of the Advisory

Body, the portion of the income to be allotted to each function of the college, carry out the policies determined upon by the Body, and select faculty and other staff members and assign their duties, in each case subject to the approval of the Body. Except during the first term of the first president, he shall be paid only the same amount of salary as the highest paid faculty member or other official or employee, but shall receive an additional amount as an expense allowance or otherwise to reimburse him for additional expenses necessitated by his duties as president. Because of the necessity for official entertaining, the Advisory Body shall assign him a house suitable for such functions or make other provision therefor.

(3) As the development of the college requires, offices may be created and filled in conformity with the principle that the time of a teaching member of the staff should be kept free for study and for teaching, and should not be encroached upon by clerical, routine, or welfare duties.

(4) The Advisory Body shall provide a retirement plan for staff members, either with or without contributions by the members.

## 8. FINANCE, ENDOWMENT, AND PLANT

BECAUSE OF CHANGES in general price level, the figures given in the following table are subject to revision.* They are presented, however, since they illustrate a *proportional* distribution of funds that would be compatible with the educational principles set forth in this prospectus.

---

* The figures given are those proposed by Dr. Cooper in 1937 Although much too low in terms of current prices, they do permit a direct comparison of the amounts allocated by him to the different items in the budget.—EDITOR.

## FINANCE

### INCOME

| | |
|---|---:|
| Income from endowment (3%) | $300,000 |
| 400 students at $400 tuition | 160,000 |
| 100 students at zero tuition* | 0 |
| Plant, dormitories, etc., operated at cost | 0 |
| Total income | $460,000 |

### EXPENDITURES

| | |
|---|---:|
| Maintenance, operation, capital outlay, reserves for equipment, etc. | $184,000 |
| Salaries of president and instruction staff and supplies of instruction | 276,000 |
| Total expenditures | $460,000 |

### ADMINISTRATION AND INSTRUCTION STAFF

| | | | |
|---|---|---|---:|
| 1 | President | | $10,000 |
| 5 | Division Heads | at $10,000 | 50,000 |
| 8 | Professors | at $7,500 | 60,000 |
| 12 | Associate Professors | at $5,000 | 60,000 |
| 11 | Assistant Professors | at $3,500 | 38,500 |
| 10 | Instructors | at $2,000 | 20,000 |
| 5 | Assistants (full-time) | at $1,500 | 7,500 |
| 10 | Secretaries of faculty members | at $1,500 | 15,000 |
| | Supplies of instruction | | 15,000 |
| | Total | | $276,000 |

## ENDOWMENT

| | |
|---|---:|
| Productive endowment | $10,000,000 |

* The remission of tuition fees shall not be based on the need of the student, but on excellence of studentship. An exception may be made in the case of entering students needing financial assistance, but such assistance will not be continued beyond the first year unless a high level of scholarship is maintained.

*PLANT*

| | |
|---|---:|
| Land, 300 acres at $50 | $15,000 |
| Library, laboratories, classrooms, health and recreation | 1,000,000 |
| Dormitories | 900,000 |
| Boys' dormitory, $500,000 | |
| Girls' dormitory, $400,000 | |
| President's residence | 15,000 |
| *Total* | $1,930,000 |

## CONCLUSION: THE COLLEGE AT A GLANCE

### Definition of Function

THE MAIN OBJECTIVE is to found and operate a small college for a highly select class of students, which shall be kept small with respect to enrollment, and shall avoid the temptation perennially to solicit donations and additions to the endowment. In order to avoid the curse that the desire for bigness entails, a maximum enrollment will be set, and that maximum will be adhered to. The college will be expected to turn out from year to year young people of high ability who have received unusual stimulation and superior instruction, and who, therefore, after having taken their professional courses or after having had experience in their nonprofessional vocations, can render society unusual service.

### Guiding Principles

(1) Graduate work as such is not to be given.

(2) No numerical minimum either of semester hours or of months of attendance is to be regarded as constituting a "college education."

(3) Degrees, as such, are not to be conferred, but recognition is to be given, either publicly or privately or both, to the acquisition of a good understanding of basic facts, theories, formulae, processes, and applications of current civilizations, customs, aspirations, resources, and techniques. This includes understanding of the various sciences, social sciences, arts, languages, religions, and philosophies. It is assumed that the

students recognized as of sufficient understanding as mentioned in the beginning of this paragraph will be certainly the mental equals or superiors of the typical university product who holds the master's degree.

(4) None of the usual devices will be resorted to for the purpose of making the student study, but no so-called student will be permitted to continue in the college. The college will be open only to those who are studious because of intellectual interest and mental curiosity, and who, because of these traits coupled with high native ability, maintain a high level of studentship and scholarship.

(5) Scholarships may be granted to entering students because of need, but no scholarship is to be either granted or continued after the first year in the college except on the merit of high studentship.

(6) Scholarship is to be constantly promoted; yet the fact is to be recognized that the best type of studentship avoids a dead grind. Therefore, a wide range of sports, games, and recreations will be made available. No one will be required to engage in any one activity, but no one will be permitted to continue in the college who does not participate in a reasonable number of them. On the other hand, intercollegiate athletics as usually promoted and practiced will not be permitted. It is the present plan to play an occasional sport or game with a team from another college, but the playing will be preceded or followed by high-grade and enjoyable social functions. The typical aspect of the contest will be absent. The individual student of Freedom College will play much more than the typical student in the typical college or university, but the wastefulness, the favoritism, the interruptions of class and laboratory work, the misplaced emphasis, and the whoop and hurrah will all be absent.

(7) The faculty members are to be selected from the very superior personnel of the institutions of higher learning in the

United States and elsewhere, from nonacademic callings, and from graduate students finishing their higher studies in universities. Since the college staff is to be made up of these superior members, and since the college cannot hold up graduate work as an incentive, the salary schedules of the universities will have to be equaled or exceeded by the college. It is expected that several teaching members of the faculty will equal any president in scholarship, outlook, resourcefulness, and general fitness. In such cases, the salaries of such teaching members will equal that of the president.

In every respect this new type of college will be expected to live up to its distinctive title of *Freedom College.*

*Part Two*

---

# OTHER ESSAYS ON EDUCATION

# EDUCATION IN THE MOST WORTH-WHILE WAY

THINKING ENABLES the world to attain new heights. Doing enables it to hold its own.

For many thousands of years the Western world made slow progress in providing itself the opportunity to live. At the end of countless ages it had attained only the elements of progress. It had domesticated animals, had converted fire into a utility, and had adapted certain food plants. It had acquired a working knowledge of some simple machines, such as the wheel and axle, the lever, and the screw; had advanced navigation by means of sailing craft to really high efficiency; had partially explored the nearer solar system; and had invented and utilized many simple instruments and tools.

Many fields of knowledge commonplace with us today remained in darkness. Little was known of the human body. Chemistry as such was unknown. Metallurgy was empirical and exceedingly rudimentary. Medicine as we know it now was a field not even glimpsed. Few natural phenomena were attributed to their real cause.

Before this condition could be changed into one more propitious, the people had to acquire not only tools with which to handle facts; but, more important, freedom to seek and use facts. Among the tools acquired were the Arabic system of notation and computation, the compass, and the telescope. Freedom was bought—mainly with blood. Since the time of Newton, freedom of thought and investigation has been rather generally enjoyed, and because of his investigation astronomy has been excluded from medical practice.

Without pausing to trace the recent changes in people's thinking and the contribution to human welfare of the great multitude of pieces of research, I shall merely mention a few:

First, medicine and sanitary engineering have lengthened the expectancy of human life in the past three and a half centuries nearly fifty years (from about 20 years in 1600 to almost 70 years in 1950).

Second, the advance in the basic sciences of biology, chemistry, and physics over the same period has made it possible to multiply farmer food production over and over.

Third, metallurgy has given us elements and combinations with qualities formerly undreamed of.

Fourth, the possibilities of knowledge or entertainment have expanded phenomenally.

Practically all of the advantages just now mentioned and those only suggested have come as the result of careful, painstaking, persistent, and penetrating thought verified by experimentation. It is true that some of them have come in part by accidental discovery or spontaneous invention; but such blessings, which may be called gifts of the gods, are few and unimportant in comparison with those bought with brains and delivered in the vigils of the laboratory. Santa Claus has brought us some things, but most of the newer advantages have been acquired on the cash-and-carry basis.

A few examples will illustrate. Leeuwenhoek spent his leisure time for months and months experimenting with lenses, and no doubt gave much thought to them even in his hours of employment. He finally produced the microscope much as we have it now, and as an immediate result became the leading biologist in the Western world. The subsequent results have been revolutionary. Because of Leeuwenhoek's work three centuries ago, we are just now transforming the field of agriculture, lengthening the span of human life, remaking the mechanic and industrial arts, and in fact discovering and exploring the microscopic world.

Again, the steam engine as given to us by Watt is sometimes described in our bedtime stories as the result of an accidental discovery followed by a spontaneous invention. The fact is that it is no such thing. So-called steam engines were in use long before Watt's time. Watt's observation of the power of steam only furnished the stimulus to thinking. He set to work to find a way to control that power. Reflection and analytical and synthetic reasoning, verified by experiment, gave us the reciprocating feature of our familiar steam engine. By means of it, industrial production and heavy transportation were revolutionized within the short period of one hundred fifty years.

Still further, the gas or internal-combustion engine had been conceived of for several decades. A number of individual physicists attempted from time to time to devise a workable engine. Success eluded them only because they could not produce a satisfactory device for igniting the fuel in the chamber. Finally, just over eighty years ago, Nikolaus Otto built the first successful four-cycle engine. Within ten years this type of engine was utilized in gasoline-powered vehicles, which started the production of modern automobiles. In the early 1890's the famous "horseless carriage," the first successful gasoline-powered automobile in America, was designed and built by the Duryea brothers.

Had not somebody hit upon the electric spark as a means of igniting fuel, there would now be no practicable automobile nor airplane nor any other machine operated by the reciprocating gas engine.

In citing the microscope, the steam engine, and electric ignition, I have given three examples of very great contributions to social welfare made by reflective and constructive thinking. If space permitted, similar cases might be cited in large numbers. The reverse might also be done. Cases might be cited of many persons who were full of energy, who influenced many people in one way or another, and who in many cases became well-to-do, but who never made a contribution either to knowledge or to procedure which improved the conditions of living. In fact, most people come in this class in all respects, unless it be in becoming well-to-do.

Why do not more people make a contribution to human welfare? That is a difficult question to answer fully.

Perhaps the best answer is that most people do not know the importance of reflective thinking. Most people cannot do thinking which can be of any consequence. Perhaps they have not been taught to do so. Perhaps they have not only not been taught to do so, but have even been taught in such a way as to prevent their learning to do so on their own initiative. Perhaps they have been kept so busy in the hours in which they were taught that they had no time to learn to think. Perhaps their elders and teachers held ability to think in such low esteem in comparison with such matters as apparent ability to memorize, conformity to approved beliefs, leadership consisting of ability to sell through emotionalism, influence through personal appeal rather than through reason—perhaps, as I said, ability to think was held in such low esteem in comparison with such traits as these as to cause most people to have a wholly erroneous estimate of its importance.

Apparently most people hold salesmanship to be much more important than scholarship. Apparently most people put entertainment far ahead of intellectual companionship. Apparently most people seek information and avoid education. Apparently most people are ardent seekers for facts but cold to their meaning.

If these conditions are not only apparent but also real, what is the cause?

Again this is a difficult question to answer. It seems, however, that the cause is clearly in the teaching which children and young people get. To be specific, we drill to fix habits without apparent reason for desiring the habits which we endeavor to fix. We drill for speed in computation and other routine, and overlook the fact that speed is desirable only for the purpose of saving time for some other activity, such as reflection. We teach facts as if they were desirable within themselves, when in reality they are worth while only when they are applied directly in life itself or in reflective thinking. We have children memorize matter, although memorizing does not necessitate the association of any meaning with the things memorized, and we fail to recognize that memory at most and at its best can do nothing more than furnish us conveniently and economically the materials with which to think. We ignore the fact that memory furnishes no meanings and points out no relationships. We teach to enable the student to pass with a higher mark a kind of test that he ought not to be required to pass at all.

What should the schools do in this matter?

The question has probably been answered already. If it has not been answered, I may say that they should throw many of their present performances into reverse. In addition to that, they should teach the students to carry on reflection and encourage them to practice it.

# SOME BASIC PRINCIPLES UNDERLYING SOUND PROCEDURES IN COLLEGE ADMINISTRATION

THE FOLLOWING PRINCIPLES, gleaned from official statements and reports made in an administrative capacity, and assembled under appropriate headings, constitute in effect a philosophy of college administration.*

## Relation to the General Public

THE welfare of the college will be determined in large measure by the attitudes which the people have toward it. Legislative action will be more favorable, more students will be attracted, a more desirable quality of student will seek to enter, the conduct of the students will be of a higher type, and monetary donations will be more likely, if the most desirable relation to the public is maintained. Means to this end are the exercise of competence, honesty, and dignity, and a liberal and helpful participation in public affairs.

## Faculty

IT SHOULD be the intention of the administration of a college to build up a faculty, each member of which is so much worth while that discontinuance of his services would be distinctly felt as a loss. Moreover, faculty co-operation should be en-

---

* The compilation of these principles has been a responsibility assumed by the Editor from the sources indicated.

couraged in building up such a staff. The proper procedure would be to cultivate and improve the staff members who show promise of improvement, and to select additions and necessary replacements with great care. While initial appointments would usually be made for one year only, the general policy should be to develop the appointee into a desirable and permanent member of the staff. It is only in really bad situations that a staff member should be discharged.

## Obligations to Students

A COLLEGE is supposed to be primarily concerned with the education of young people. Instability and lack of purpose in the management of an institution prevent the orderly processes essential to the proper instruction of the young. When a student registers at a college, there are implicit in that registration certain educational rights which the college authorities have no right to withhold or deny, nor do they have a right to introduce distractions or uncertainties which destroy these rights.

## Finances

As A DISTINCTION between a business venture and an educational institution, it may be said that persons are justified in speculative ventures in business when they exercise the best judgment they have, and many of these ventures turn out well and make great contributions to the welfare of society. In contrast, the education of youth, while always susceptible to slight modification, is stabilized to a degree that anything approaching speculation in connection with it is inappropriate. A college, therefore, that cannot over a period of years handle its affairs in such a way as to get along without repudiation of debts cannot justify its existence. Moreover, reputable American colleges do not operate on income from fees alone.

## Accreditation

ACCREDITING AGENCIES have come in recent years to study carefully the financial operations of colleges. Sound budgetary procedures have been devised and applied. Before being accredited, an institution has to bring its financial affairs into the open and must be employing a budgetary procedure that commends itself to the commission.

Without considering specific requirements, it may be pointed out that accreditation can be facilitated (*a*) by getting the reputation of doing a good job, (*b*) by avoidance of extravagant statements commendatory of the college, (*c*) by concealing nothing, but on the contrary answering freely all questions asked by competent authority, (*d*) by confining statements of information to verifiable fact, and (*e*) by expressing opinion as opinion and not as fact.

## Definition of Functions

THE STAFF are frequently uncertain and are therefore hampered in their work by not having at hand for reference a body of the rules, restrictions, and policy of the administration. These should be compiled, and put in the hands of such officers as the president, the dean, the business manager, the registrar, and the deans of women and of men.

These rules should, among other things, define clearly the functions of these officers and differentiate their fields, so that each may know when he is performing his own functions and where the field that has been assigned to some other officer begins.

## Publicity

OBVIOUSLY, if publicity has any influence in attracting students, the kind of student attracted by it will depend upon the quality of the publicity. If the releases reveal earnestness, a recognition of responsibility, a commendable purpose, and a true sense of proportion, one kind of student will be attracted. If, on the other hand, the releases reflect a lackadaisical attitude, frivolous purposes, a distorted notion of relative values, or a tendency to magnify the unimportant, then another type of student will be attracted. To the end that publicity may consistently promote the best interests of the college, it should be centralized and the central authority should handle it judiciously at all times.

### Stability

SOME ELEMENTS implying stability in an institution may be mentioned briefly. Retention of staff is obviously one of these, and is in fact the evidence of stability most readily observed by outsiders. Others are perhaps equally important. Discipline should be steady. Curriculum offerings should be consistent and continuous. Plant operations should be workman-like and permanent. Increase in student members should be kept in hand, should be steady, and should not be permitted to become spectacular. All large changes should be thoroughly considered well in advance of their initiation. Moreover, any proposed change, to merit consideration, should be thoroughly sound educationally.

In conclusion, it may be said that a college worthy of continuance is one that is honest with its clientele, and is able to attract an administrative and teaching staff who sustain unquestioned integrity as individuals; is one in which the physical plant and the corporate entity of the college are removed from the realm of real-estate speculation and chicanery; is one which has so established itself financially and otherwise that the administrative and instructional staffs are relieved of anxiety and worry and have both time and intelligence released and made available for real educational endeavor; and, finally, is one which conducts its affairs in such a way as to merit the confidence, support, and co-operation of the community, the alumni, and all others of the region who are interested in the civic and educational well-being of the people.

# THE DIFFERING OBJECTIVES OF GENERAL EDUCATION AND PROFESSIONAL EDUCATION AND SOME PRACTICAL APPLICATIONS

GENERAL EDUCATION may be regarded as any education that enables one to observe, practice, appreciate, or understand observable phenomena, whether they be in the field of nature or of organized society, or in the purely intellectual realm. Professional education, in contrast, is that which enables one to practice a profession.

A person may be regarded as having at least attained to a low degree of general education, regardless of his level of general intelligence, even though his observations be inaccurate, his enjoyment meager, and his understanding confused. To be able to practice a profession satisfactorily, however, the person practicing it must be able to observe accurately, enjoy adequately, and understand clearly. In addition to this, he must have the knowledge and skill frequently and immediately applicable to the profession he practices.

It is assumed by many, including many students, that the only difference between the person of general education and the one of professional education consists in the professional knowledge and skill just now mentioned. It is true that a person is found now and then whose general education is so extensive and so thorough that, if the professional were added, he would be well equipped to practice in a professional field. Such persons, however, are rare.

The distinction between the school which has as its function the provision of general education and that which provides professional education is this:

The school which provides general education enables the individual to develop whatever talent or aptitude he may have, whether the amount be much or little. The criterion of classification and promotion should be where, in the judgment of the staff, the student can do most for himself. Thus a dull child may know little of the material of the grade in which he is at any one time, but if, in the opinion of the staff, he can do more for himself in a grade more advanced he should be assigned to that grade. Promotion or graduation in such a school does not certify or even assure any considerable knowledge of the contents of the grades passed over. Graduation, for example, signifies that the student has been a citizen of the group, that his behavior was such that he could be tolerated, and that the staff has been of the opinion that he has become about saturated at each successive level.

The school which provides professional education, on the other hand, by graduating the candidate certifies not only that his behavior has been tolerable, but likewise that he knows the field and can operate in it sufficiently well to justify the client or the public in entrusting him with matters in that field. In the case of a teachers' college, the student is at all times passing a teachers' examination. Every course is a partial teachers' examination, and all his acts which are observed outside of classrooms are partial teachers' examinations. Graduation is certification of that candidate for the practice of teaching.

The primary function of the teachers' college, therefore, is not to enable the student to become saturated at one level and to advance to another. On the contrary, it is to see to it that he has the opportunity to acquire proficiency in a field, and (no less important) to decline to pass him unless he unquestionably attains to that proficiency. The burden of proof is always on the student, and all doubtful cases should fail to pass.

I have discussed this subject repeatedly with students and with faculty members. Students rather generally approve, but wonder what the application of the principle involved would do to them. Faculty members generally approve, but regret that teachers' colleges have never seriously approached the application of the principle.

I recognize that this principle would not work well at first if put into operation abruptly. However, it should be uppermost in the minds of teachers' college staffs, and a college which seeks to provide professional education for teachers should move consistently toward its application.

Steps to improve the level of professional education in our teachers' colleges might include the following:

1. Release the teaching members of the staff from much of their semi-welfare work, and give them a chance to gratify their scholastic interests. As it is, faculty members in general use the library too little, not in their own fields alone, but their knowledge gained from general reading should be expanded.
2. Build up in our students a conscientiousness with respect to *accuracy* and *fullness* of knowledge, and cause them to be sensitive to the fact that inaccurate knowledge may be deceptive, and that a little knowledge may seem to support erroneous conclusions which full knowledge would contradict. Again, it must be pointed out that our students not only use the library too little, but certain classes of books, such as compendia of facts, yearbooks, abstracts, and encyclopedias, are practically unknown to them.
3. Broaden the outlook of our students by introducing them to the intriguing aspects of a variety of the more exacting nonprofessional courses of wide application. So far we have failed to show them that every subject taught in the curriculum—

economics, statistics, physiology, chemistry, physics, to name only a few—has romance either in its application or in its history.

In instituting such changes, no definite equipment would be required. What would be required is a full recognition of need with perhaps some additions to the library.

# THE COST OF EXTRA-TEACHING ACTIVITIES
# OF COLLEGE FACULTIES

THE FACULTY of the typical American college that is purely an undergraduate school is expected, besides its teaching and preparation for teaching, to do a considerable amount in the aggregate of non-teaching and, it may be, non-scholastic work. These demands consist of disciplinary, welfare, clerical and semi-clerical, and other functions more or less routine, in addition to attendance upon faculty and assembly meetings.

The amount of time required to satisfy the demands made by the mere routine and superficial functions ranges from very high in some schools to very low in others. Records of time so spent are very meager and, where they exist, of questionable accuracy. If timecards covering such demands are kept in any school, the process used in this discussion may be applied and the cost of each function thereby determined.

The process will be illustrated by considering the time presumably spent in assembly and in faculty meetings in a certain college over a one-year period, because these demands are definite and involve the whole faculty, and therefore consume considerable time. If the time assumed in this illustration to have been spent in these ways was not actually so spent, in that case there was a miscarriage of plans; but the process of cost accounting does not assume in this case such a miscarriage.

Reeves and Russell* in their formula for computing faculty

* Floyd W. Reeves and J. J. Russell, *College Organization and Administration*, Ch. VIII.

load assign both to teaching hours and to preparations a weight that in the application of the formula in each case becomes one-fourth of the full weight of the load, without regard to the number of students involved, thus totaling one-half for these activities combined. To the number of students per staff member is assigned the remaining one-half. These gentlemen do not consider such activities as assembly and faculty meetings, but in order to determine the cost of faculty time devoted to these activities, they are here treated, hour for hour, the same as teaching or preparation.

*Data for Calculating the Costs*
*of Selected Extra-Teaching Activities of a College Faculty*
*on an Annual Basis*

| | | |
|---|---:|---:|
| Total current cost | | $300,432.48 |
| Faculty salary cost | | $174,993.10 |
| Total teaching hours | 24,311 | |
| Total hours of preparation by staff | 20,318 | |
| Total hours of staff spent in assembly meetings | 4,635 | |
| Total hours of staff spent in faculty meetings | 1,404 | |
| Total hours of staff time (last four items) | | 50,668 |
| Number of assembly meetings of one hour | | 120* |
| Number of faculty meetings of one hour | | 36 |

* The number of assembly meetings was in reality 240 and the period was half an hour in length.

The foregoing tabulation shows 50,668 hours devoted to teaching, preparation, assembly, and faculty meetings. Of this time, assembly claims 9.15 per cent, faculty meetings 2.77 per cent, and the two together 11.92 per cent. The cost of faculty time spent in assembly for the year, therefore, is one-half of 9.15 per cent of $300,432.48, or $13,744.79. The cost of faculty time spent in faculty meetings is one-half of 2.77

per cent of $300,432.48, or $4,160.99. The cost of the two is accordingly $17,905.78.

The figures given further indicate that the 120 assembly meetings and the 36 faculty meetings cost $114.54 and $115.58, respectively, per meeting.*

Each college administration would do well to answer for itself the question as to whether such extra-teaching activities justify themselves in terms of cost accounting.

---

* In explanation of the difference in the cost of the two kinds of meetings, it may be stated that the faculty meetings ran only through the semesters, whereas the assembly meetings were continued throughout the year, the average size of the staff being somewhat larger during the semesters.

# WHITHER ATHLETICS?

THE COMING SCHOLASTIC YEAR will probably experience about the usual number of tempests in teapots, the ebullition being caused by athletics. It is to be expected that the months to follow will repeat the history of past years.

Colleges A, B, and C will boil, and Colleges D, E, and F will calm the troubled waters by announcing with grave piety that they have quit winning disastrously with a few students but have arranged to lose successfully with their whole studentry. The tempests of A, B, and C will subside, leaving no evidence of violence except a few pieces of linen, some private and some official, that must be washed. The *reforms* announced by D, E, and F will likewise subside, leaving no trace, if indeed a resurgence ever took place.

The public will look on. A few persons will reflect. Of the others, some will get "het up," while the great majority will be entirely unimpressed, and will be concerned only with the probability of getting tickets to future games and with the hope of making a little "jack" on the wise side.

The thoughts of those who reflect are a matter of some concern, for the mere fact that they do reflect indicates that they observe social movements and are desirous of promoting the best. They might reflect on other phenomena than athletics, did athletics not obtrude itself.

Athletics shouts for attention through the daily press; through the uproar on the bleachers; through the " 'thuse"; through the marring of buildings and sidewalks by zealous fans with paintbrushes in their hands; through conversation and contention in clubs, smoking rooms, and elsewhere; through government by way of tax bills; through quasi-government by way of subscriptions and donations to stadium, alumni, and other funds; through parenthood of college students by way of the activities fee assessed at the time of registration; through the attitudes fixed or attempted by means of "chapel" devoted to "pep," and by other means intended to supply the bone to the bone and sinew in the ranks that support "Old Siwash"; and, finally, through the buildings and equipment on the campus.

All the means of obtruding may be passed without comment except the last. If the observer may judge by equipment, the purposes of the colleges are so diverse as to indicate the absence of any large interest common to all. On the one hand are those that give evidence of proceeding on the assumption that the important things in a college career have a vital relation to laboratories, library, classrooms, and facilities for recreation, including coherent expression of ideas and their exchange with fellow human beings. On the other hand are those that make the physical the big feature, as evidenced by the distribution of funds for buildings, equipment, and grounds. Colleges G, H, I, J, K, and L are typical of this class.

College G, a state institution of mongrel type, teacher-training and liberal arts, has a gymnasium costing $250,000 and an athletic field costing $30,000, as compared with a library building and materials costing $80,000. H, a college of the same kind, has a stadium costing $250,000 and a gymnasium costing $250,000, as compared with a library building costing $250,000 and materials costing $50,000. I, a state university, has a gymnasium costing $210,000 and a stadium costing $300,000, with a library and materials costing $100,000. J, another state university, has a gymnasium costing $280,000 and a stadium costing $450,000, with a library and materials costing

$65,000. K, a private university subsidized by the state, has a gymnasium valued at $315,000 and an athletic field costing $200,000, with a library consisting of one reading room in one of the university buildings and books anywhere in niches and corners, the whole being worth perhaps $75,000. L, a state university, has a stadium costing $500,000, occupying land worth probably $50,000, with a library building worth $100,000 and materials worth probably an equal amount.

All of these universities affect graduate instruction, and J and K confer the degree of Doctor of Philosophy. K is an institution of about 3,000 students that spends $125,000 on a football season, but does not own or rent even one tennis court. It provides no means of physical play except those already mentioned, and does not have a theatre, a parlor, a clubroom, or any other facility designed to provide mental recreation.

It was said that University L has a stadium. To be exact, it should be stated that the university merely gives range privileges on the public domain to a syndicate which runs a stadium on the campus throughout the year. (The weather is mild in that region even in winter, and the stadium crowd is a hardy breed.) The university does not have control of admissions, but, on the contrary, occupancy is divided among the members of the syndicate. While some of the detail is not known to the writer, yet it seems that the university is not indemnified by the syndicate against liability in case of collapse or other mishap, nor did the syndicate provide a guarantee that it would complete the stadium when once begun, or remove the debris created in the attempt to build, in the event of failure. This case is the most naïve and unseemly occupancy of public property which the writer has ever known to be sanctioned by public officers.

All of the institutions listed from G to L, except K, provide some means of sport such as tennis courts.

So much for what one sees when one observes. Can one judge by observation what the purpose of the American college is? The situation calls to mind the story of the rejected suitor who bravely faced a positive negative, strode from the room, mounted his horse, and rode away in every direction.

In this maze of practice and wilderness of purpose there are some college administrators looking for a plan—some evidently desire a plan to follow on their way out, and others, it would seem, would be quite content with a plan that would serve as a subject for faculty legislation and presidential proclamation. A review of the salient facts as the observer sees them may suggest a feasible plan to those looking for guidance. Whatever the facts may appear to be to one on the inside, to one on the outside they seem to be these:

1.  Might makes merit. The husky of the family of games, football, has taken to itself the playing grounds, locker rooms, shower baths, the time of coaches, both the fall and the spring seasons, and whatever else it desired. It has induced its friends to build costly stadia for its accommodation. The other games in the family must content themselves with whatever it does not care to use. It provides them hush money in irregular amounts at irregular times.
2.  Basketball is cultivated somewhat as a green manure or cover crop to keep the soil in condition in the fallow period. Baseball, tennis, and winter, aquatic, and minor sports have been practically dispossessed.
3.  Football to all intents and purposes is an institution apart from the organism called the college. The name of the college is used in speaking of the institution to signify the geographic location of its activities and vaguely to designate its clientele.
4.  Football is growing more and more costly. For that reason it is a heavy financial load in the out-of-the-way places. In the large centers, on the contrary, it should if well managed be

enormously profitable, because of the large gate and other
receipts. In localities that are neither out-of-the-way nor
metropolitan it may or may not be remunerative.

5. There is a tendency among colleges so situated that football
   is unprofitable to assess a fee against the student at registration to cover activities, including athletic games, the student
   not being consulted as to whether he is interested in the
   activities or not. The attitude is one of take it or leave it.
   There is a tendency, equally marked, not to include football
   in the activities covered by the fee in colleges located where
   football is profitable. In most colleges the students are
   solemnly and ardently exhorted to attend *en masse* and help
   win the game for alma mater.

6. The intercollegiate as well as the intra-college legislation ad-
   dresses itself to restriction and to limiting the game, reducing
   the number of years in which an individual may play, and
   restricting an institution to minutely prescribed competitors—
   discrediting the game by attempts to reduce rather than
   add to the amount of playing to be done.

7. At irregular intervals a charge of professionalism is made. It
   is vigorously denied, and a countercharge of soreheadedness
   or ulterior motive is made. A counterdenial immediately
   follows. Neither charge nor countercharge is supported by
   tangible evidence. The denial of the charge is supported by
   vehemence and official dignity only. A financial accounting
   is not made public. Charge, countercharge, denial, and
   counterdenial are futile and unconvincing.

8. With regard to honesty and integrity of management the
   public regards football in precisely the same way as it does
   the typical circus with its sideshows and concessions. In fact,
   the people have so little confidence in the integrity of the
   management that their distrust would be ruinous to many
   businesses. The banker or the dairyman would have to go out
   of business if he could not command a higher degree of
   confidence. At the games the public safeguards its financial
   interests by counting its change carefully, and seats itself
   as an amused spectator of a spectacular fraud.

9. The season covers about six games. The preparation occupies a few days or weeks in the spring and a somewhat longer period in the fall preceding the first game, and continues through the season, which ends about Thanksgiving Day.
10. The game is legislated, restricted, standardized, coached, equipped, advertised, commercialized, and spectated until it is no longer a game, but instead is a laborious response to the orders of the foreman.

If the ten statements offered above embody substantially the facts, there would seem to be four distinct procedures, any one of which might be followed. In any one of the four the practice may be defended more or less successfully.

1. Make no organic change. Go on according to the plan now in vogue.
2. Subsidize openly, and let such other changes come about as are inherent in such a plan.
3. Abolish admission fees to games and let consequent changes take place.
4. Abolish official coaches, managerships, records, trophy museums, and other appurtenances to highly organized competition.

Little need be said about the first plan. If it seems to be reasonably satisfactory there is no adequate reason for change. The reason for discussing the subject is the apparent dissatisfaction with the system.

Even if this plan justifies its continuance, public interest would be stimulated, confidence where merited would be strengthened, and much gossip would be allayed by a financial statement published periodically in considerable detail. It may be objected that the financial management of such enterprises is no part of the business of the public. Such an objection is difficult to sustain, for the college makes a continuous appeal to the public for both moral and financial support. Any organization that appeals to the public for support by so doing makes itself a quasi-public organization, and as such should account for that support, be it moral or financial. The mere fact that the college is tax-exempt in its plant, income, endowment, and donations justifies such an accounting.

It may be objected again that where profits are shown by the statement to be large, other organizations would be encouraged to compete by undertaking rival athletic enterprises. To meet that objection it need only be stated that the college enjoys a monopoly of its name even when applied to athletics. Besides that, any attempt at business competition would probably be construed by the students and other friends as aggression and would result in a solidarity of support that is now lacking.

The second plan, if embarked upon, would not change matters materially, since in the opinion of the public it would not differ from the first plan except in the degree of openness.

The chief advantages of the change would probably be to put the entering athlete who is conscientious at equal advantage with others, to enable the individual student to ascertain his real selling value, to bring about a less costly program of athletics for the college that needs it, to lengthen the season, to improve in the minds of the people the standing of the members of the staff having to do directly or indirectly with athletics, and to remove the incentive to gossip.

Baseball, by exposing its graft a number of years ago and attempting in subsequent years not only to be clean in its operation but also to have only clean men on its teams, has taken a place in the estimation of the people to which college athletics might well aspire. Professionalism in professional baseball is not objectionable to the public. It may seem inappropriate for the college to carry on professional sport. Experience might show that it is actually inappropriate. On the surface it does not seem so. The college does not hesitate to employ for pay professional talent in music and drama for the entertainment of the public and does not object if some of these entertainers happen to be its own students. Again, the college has a consistent practice of employing its own students as assistants in the various libraries, offices, and laboratories. It would seem, then, that the only real objection to employing professional athletes is the element of competition which still bears the name and has the superficial aspect of intercollegiate contest. This objection wilts, in the light of present-day realism, into fiction. As was said before, hardier objections might develop in the light of experience.

The third plan, the abolition of admission fees, has many possibilities for good and for ill. Experience would no doubt reveal many. Some that can be foreseen somewhat clearly are these:

1. There would be a drastic decline in revenue from athletics.
2. The cost of equipment, regalia, travel, and other adjuncts and concomitants would decline.
3. The attractiveness of athletics as a field of exploitation would be greatly changed and somewhat reduced.
4. The student would not be greatly influenced in important decisions by the money value of his playing ability.
5. Fewer people would play because of external incentives.
6. Relatively more would play because of the inherent merit of the game.
7. A much wider variety of games would be played on the campus.
8. The spectator of games would come to feel that he is the guest of the college, and not, as now, exercising a right fully paid for. The change of attitude would probably change the conduct both of host and of guest.
9. The prospect of the "gate" would cease to influence the selection of the teams to be met as competitors.
10. The sport element would be greatly augmented.

The fourth plan, if applied, would merely initiate a return to *Jeffersonian principles* or to the Garden of Eden of athletic sports. Such a plan would virtually say to students:

"The college approves sports, and hopes that you will engage in them to the utmost that is consistent with your purposes as young individuals and the demands that those purposes make on your time and energy. It is not feasible for you to provide yourselves with playing fields and floors, nor even with suits and other equipment. All of these things are furnished by the college, but you must not abuse any of them, and must care for your suits and other individual equipment according to specifications which experience has shown to be desirable and at the same time not burdensome. The specifications include the care of suits and other garments when removed after the play for the day is finished, the necessary cleaning of suits from time to time, and the cleaning and oiling of shoes and other leather equipment. The college will repossess at once the entire equipment of any student who neglects any part of it. (You understand, of course, that the college provides you with these things out of funds which you or your friends pay into the treasury in the form of incidental, athletic, or tuition fees, or as donations.)

"You may play as often as your time will permit, and may play any game at any season of the year. We have staff members who can show you how to play well. Call upon them for instruction. They will not coach you in the sense of commanding, but will teach you.

"You may have contests in the various sports with any individuals or teams who are clean enough to be safe from the standpoint of health and who conduct themselves in such a way as to be tolerable. They need not be students. You may invite groups to the campus to play, and you may furnish them rooms and meals and give them a party if you desire to do so.

"You may go away to play. When you go, you will pay your expenses. The college will send a staff member along at its expense. He will help you if you need help, and in case of misconduct on the part of any student of the college he will take charge of the offender. He will not manage the team, nor will he *coach* it, but he will give suggestions if asked to do so. You will probably not need this staff member, but he will be there to serve you in the event of your needing him. When you make trips for sport it is hoped that you will enjoy them. You will have entire freedom except as limited by the dignity and decorum of worth-while studentship.

"The college will keep no records of scores in games and will maintain no roster of players, nor will it house trophies. The record of each student will carry entries sufficiently full to give useful information as to the amount of his participation in physical sports and other recreational and athletic activities, and the degree of his proficiency in them."

Among these four plans the third and fourth have the advantage of promising very much more play than either of the others. The plan in operation now affords very little play, but imposes much work. It should be recognized that drill on the part of a game is not play but work.

# WHAT OUGHT THE PEOPLE TO DO WITH THE COLLEGES?

THE PEOPLE—all the people—depend upon the colleges. They look to them not only to train future leaders but for direct leadership in many vital matters. A large percentage of the authorities in all lines of knowledge are in the institutions of higher learning. If these institutions are to produce authorities in the future, they must guard their standards of work and scholarship very carefully. Since the people are vitally concerned, they would unquestionably be spurred to action, if they knew the conditions prevailing. Many of the colleges of liberal arts and most of the teachers' colleges are wholly supported by the states. They are a part of the states. The people evidently wanted college work done; otherwise they would have established some other kind of schools instead of colleges. In the case of the teachers' colleges, the people in converting them seem to have expected college work to be done, but for lack of information did not provide the facilities necessary to a college.

Just what is the situation with regard to the colleges?

1. The growth of the student enrollment has far outstripped that of the college faculties.
2. The number entering college is far below what it ought to be, although, by the prevailing methods of selection for admission, some enter who, because of low ability, give no promise of success.
3. An adequate number of faculty members has not been provided, and in some instances scholarship in the faculties has been diluted.
4. Some of the so-called colleges have not yet become colleges

except in name. For a number of years this was especially true of the teachers' colleges which were originally established as normal schools.

What can be done to correct these conditions?

1. Permit the persons of high ability to move as rapidly as their ability will sustain them in the elementary and high schools and in the college. This will enable them to get through college at an age early enough that many of them will feel that they can afford to take the time to study in and even through a graduate school.
2. Select the good abilities while in the elementary and high schools and bring them up with the idea of a higher education as a part of their habitual thinking. Ways should be provided to make it financially possible for all of these good abilities to develop themselves.
3. Make college teaching attractive as a profession so that a large part of the good abilities will prepare for it and enter upon it. Some of the means to this end are (*a*) remuneration commensurate with the ability and preparation required, (*b*) freedom from politics within the institution, (*c*) academic freedom, and (*d*) opportunity for research by partial release from teaching and by subsidy.
4. While giving encouragement, financial and otherwise, to prospective students who give promise of success, decline to admit, even on trial, those of intelligence too low to be promising, especially in the case of institutions for the professional education of teachers.
5. In the colleges of liberal arts, and even more in the teachers' colleges, apportion the money provided in such a way as to give relatively more for instruction—salaries of faculty and supplies and equipment for instruction—and relatively less for buildings. It seems that people want to see physical things like buildings. They are much more willing to give money for buildings than for salaries of faculty. For this reason, while

the colleges are not even well provided with buildings, they are much less well provided with money with which to provide good instruction.

6. The executives of the teachers' colleges must recognize that calling an institution a college does not make it one—that it is one thing to blossom out into a college and another thing to blossom out into the name of college. The most important element in a college is the faculty. The teachers' colleges are understaffed. Mere numbers can be added at any time, but it must be recognized that years of training are required to prepare well-equipped faculty members at the college level.

This essay has concerned itself with the colleges of liberal arts and those for the preparation of teachers. The reasons for including the teachers' colleges are (1) a considerable number of students use them as liberal arts colleges by studying in them with no apparent expectation of teaching, and (2) the output of these schools exerts a very potent influence in the determination of educational policy throughout the country.

Unfortunately, some of the shortcomings of the colleges discussed also characterize a number of other types of colleges for professional education throughout the country.

# WHO SHOULD ASPIRE TO COLLEGE TEACHING?

Who should aspire to college teaching?

Those who have a love of learning.

Those who have ability to learn.

Those who have endurance in application to large matters and also to details.

Those who have ability to differentiate values.

Those who value scholarship above salesmanship.

Those who are willing to lead a settled financial life and sustain themselves on a moderate income.

Those who are willing to pay the price of specialized study aggregating several years before beginning their careers of college teaching.

Those who hold ability to think in such high esteem that they will endeavor to teach students how to carry on reflective thinking, and will encourage them to practice it.